An Eye on Spiders

Tarantulas

by Kristine Spanier

Bullfrog Books

Ideas for Parents and Teachers

Bullfrog Books let children practice reading informational text at the earliest reading levels. Repetition, familiar words, and photo labels support early readers.

Before Reading

• Discuss the cover photo. What does it tell them?

• Look at the picture glossary together. Read and discuss the words.

Read the Book

• "Walk" through the book and look at the photos. Let the child ask questions. Point out the photo labels.

• Read the book to the child, or have him or her read independently.

After Reading

• Prompt the child to think more. Ask: Does it surprise you that so many colors of tarantulas exist? What other blue and pink creatures have you found in nature?

Bullfrog Books are published by Jump!
5357 Penn Avenue South
Minneapolis, MN 55419
www.jumplibrary.com

Library of Congress Cataloging-in-Publication Data

Names: Spanier, Kristine, author.
Title: Tarantulas / by Kristine Spanier.
Description: Minneapolis, MN : Jump!, Inc., [2018]
Series: Bullfrog Books. An eye on spiders
"Bullfrog Books are published by Jump!"
Audience: Ages 5–8. | Audience: K to grade 3.
Includes bibliographical references and index.
Identifiers: LCCN 2017041222 (print)
LCCN 2017043182 (ebook)
ISBN 9781624967955 (e-book)
ISBN 9781624967948 (hardcover : alk. paper)
Subjects: LCSH: Tarantulas—Juvenile literature.
Spiders—Juvenile literature.
Classification: LCC QL458.42.T5 (ebook)
LCC QL458.42.T5 S63 2018 (print) | DDC 595.4/4—dc23
LC record available at https://lccn.loc.gov/2017041222

Editor: Jenna Trnka
Book Designer: Molly Ballanger

Photo Credits: Olgysha/Shutterstock, cover; pets in frames/Shutterstock, 1; Karolina Chaberek/ Shutterstock, 3; Cathy Keifer/Shutterstock, 4, 12–13; Lynn M. Stone/Minden, 5, 23bl; Frank B Yuwono/ Shutterstock, 6–7; Petra Wegner/Alamy, 8, 23br; Mark Moffett/Minden, 9; xtotha/Shutterstock, 10–11, 24; blickwinkel/Alamy, 14; Nick Garbutt/Nature Picture Library, 15; Aleksey Stemmer/Shutterstock, 16–17l, 22; Thierry Montford/age fotostock, 16–17r; Ian Beames/Ardea/Biosphoto, 18–19, 23tl; Kenneth M Highfill/Science Source, 20–21, 23tr.

Printed in the United States of America at Corporate Graphics in North Mankato, Minnesota.

Table of Contents

Big and Hairy 4

Where in the World? 22

Picture Glossary 23

Index 24

To Learn More 24

West Elementary School
920 King St.
Spearfish, SD 57783

Big and Hairy

A tarantula lies
on his back.

He sheds his exoskeleton.

It was too small.

exoskeleton

It is dark.

It is time to hunt.

They eat insects.

insect

8

What else?

Mice and frogs.

Tarantulas live in holes.
They find them.
Or they dig new ones.

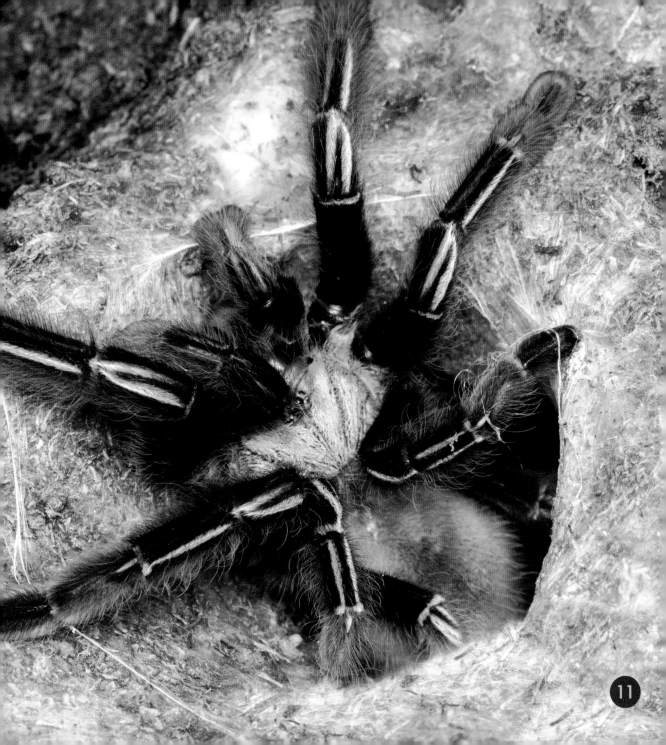

There are 900 kinds
of tarantulas.

Fine hair covers them.

Most are black and brown.
But there are other colors.
Some are blue!

14

This one is pink!

Some are as big
as an adult hand.

Others are more
than twice as big!

egg sac

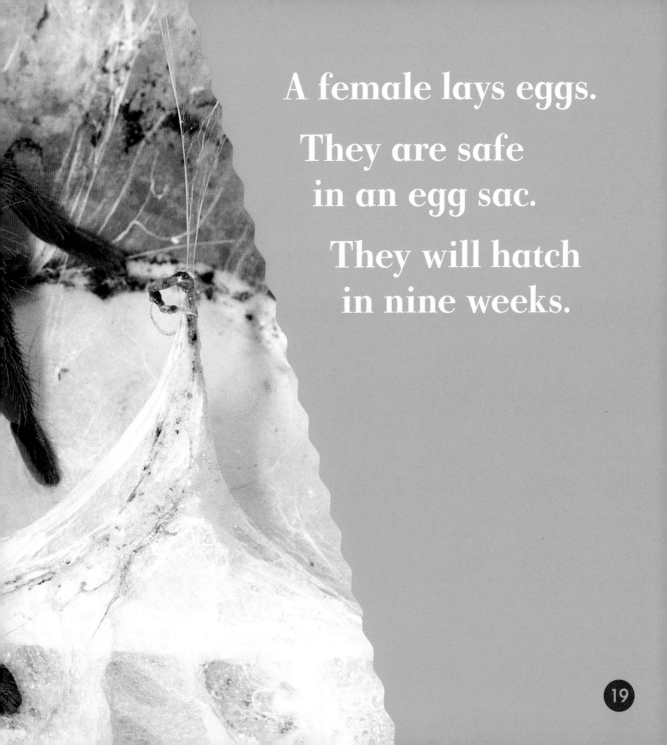

A female lays eggs.
They are safe
in an egg sac.
They will hatch
in nine weeks.

They will move
away and grow.

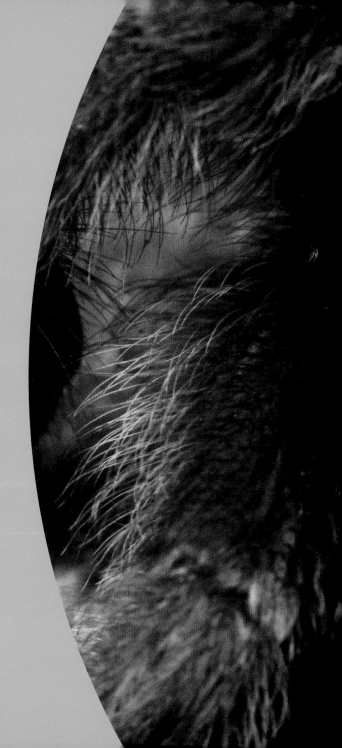

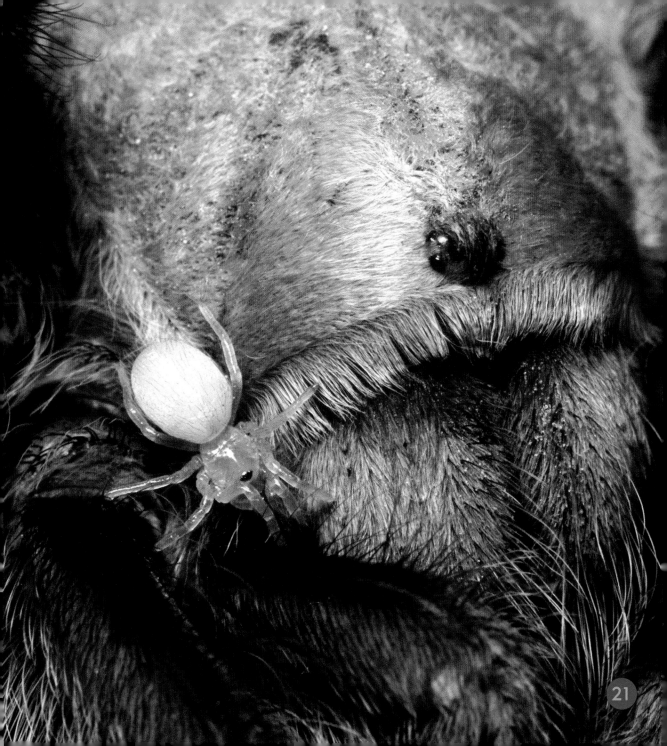

Where in the World?

Tarantulas live in tropical and desert areas around the world.

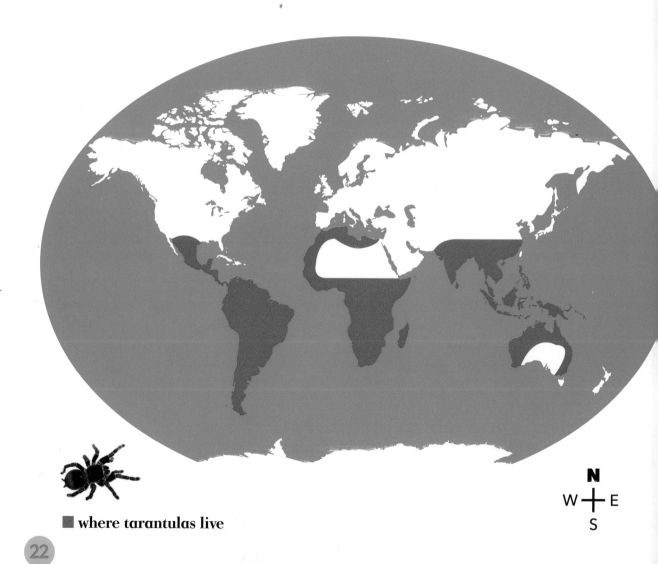

■ where tarantulas live

N
W — E
S

Picture Glossary

egg sac
A protective pouch in which a female spider lays her eggs.

hatch
To emerge from an egg.

exoskeleton
The hard outer covering that protects an animal's soft body.

insects
Small creatures with wings, six legs, and three main body parts.

Index

colors 14

eggs 19

egg sac 19

exoskeleton 5

frogs 9

hair 13

hatch 19

holes 10

hunt 7

insects 8

kinds 13

mice 9

To Learn More

Learning more is as easy as 1, 2, 3.

1) Go to www.factsurfer.com

2) Enter "tarantulas" into the search box.

3) Click the "Surf" button to see a list of websites.

With factsurfer.com, finding more information is just a click away.